W9-BAN-209

Top of the Charts

Pam Cardiff

SCHOLASTIC INC.
New York Toronto London Auckland Sydney
Mexico City New Delhi Hong Kong

Cover photo credits
Ricky Martin: ©AFP/Corbis;
Christina Aguilera: ©Black & Toby/Corbis-Sygma;
Backstreet Boys: ©Ethan Mill/Corbis

Copyright © 2001 by Scholastic Inc.
All rights reserved. Published by Scholastic Inc.
Printed in the U.S.A.

ISBN 0-439-31287-6

SCHOLASTIC, READ 180, and associated logos and designs are trademarks and/or registered trademarks of Scholastic Inc.
LEXILE is a trademark of MetaMetrics, Inc.

6 7 8 9 10   40   11 12 13 14/0

Contents

Introduction

What do Ricky Martin, Will Smith, and Madonna have in common?

Well, for one thing, they're super talented. They're also good-looking. They dress with style. And they have millions of adoring fans.

Ricky, Will, and Madonna are pop stars who have made it to the top of the charts.

Photo: AP Photo/Mark J. Terrill

Will Smith performs before 70,000 fans at Dodger Stadium in Los Angeles. The 1999 concert featured 12 acts, including Ricky Martin and Britney Spears.

What is it that makes these pop stars so special? This book takes a look at some of the biggest stars over the years. You'll find out how they got to the top. How they deal with fame. And what makes them tick.

So what are you waiting for?

Stars Are Born

"Everybody, let's rock."
—"JAILHOUSE ROCK" SUNG BY ELVIS PRESLEY

The 1950s are remembered as a happy time for many people in the U.S. World War II was over. People had jobs. They had money to spend. The radio played lots of happy songs. Older people liked this cheerful music. Their children thought it was boring. These kids wanted to listen to something more exciting. Their wish was about to come true.

A new kind of music was being born. People were mixing country and folk with rhythm and blues. They plugged in their guitars, and a D.J. called the new sound "rock and roll."

Elvis Presley

Elvis Presley was born in 1935 in Mississippi. Elvis's family did not have a lot of money.

As a young man, Elvis was a truck driver. But he loved to sing. He listened to country music, rhythm and blues, and gospel.

One day he had an idea. On his lunch hour, he walked into Sun Records in Memphis, Tennessee. He recorded two songs. They were a birthday present for his mother.

The people at Sun Records liked Elvis's sound. By the next year, he had a record **contract** with Sun.

Elvis had talent and good looks. He also had a special style. He looked cool. He acted tough. He shook his hips when he danced.

One night Elvis was scheduled to sing on *The Ed Sullivan Show*. It was the most popular TV show in the country. But Sullivan was afraid some people might not like the way Elvis moved. So, he had Elvis filmed from the waist up only. Almost one out of every three Americans watched Elvis that night. But they

Elvis Presley rehearses for his appearance on the Ed Sullivan Show on October 28, 1956.

didn't see him shake his hips!

Elvis's fame grew and grew. He had lots of hit songs, like "Hound Dog," "Love Me Tender," and "Jailhouse Rock." He starred in many movies, too. Fans called him "The King of Rock and Roll." Elvis remained a star until he died in 1977.

Today, fans still visit his home in Graceland, Tennesee. Some fans refuse to believe that Elvis really died. Some claim to have seen him still alive.

Another teen idol of the 50s might also have become a superstar. But his life was cut short before he got the chance.

Ritchie Valens

At the age of five, Ritchie Valenzuela made his first guitar out of a cigar box and string. He carried it wherever he went.

When he was in junior high, Ritchie's mother bought him an old guitar. Ritchie took it to school. He fixed it up in wood shop. He painted it green and white. He played it for anyone who would listen.

Photo: © Bettmann/Corbis

Ritchie Valens died before he could become a superstar.

Soon Ritchie was playing in local bands. A record executive heard him, and offered him a contract. He was only 16 years old. Ritchie's manager changed Ritchie's last name to Valens. Then Ritchie made his first single, "Come On Let's Go." The record was a big hit. Soon Ritchie had fans all over the U.S.

Ritchie's next record was an even bigger hit. Ritchie wrote it for his high school sweetheart, Donna Ludwig. The song was called "Donna." On the other side of the record was an old Mexican wedding song. It was called "La Bamba." Ritchie gave it a rock and roll beat. It was an even bigger hit. At the age of 17, Ritchie Valens was a teen idol.

Then one night, Ritchie was on tour. The tour bus broke down. It was freezing cold and late. Buddy Holly, another singer on the tour, hired an airplane. The plane would take Holly, Ritchie, and a third singer called "The Big Bopper" to their next show.

The plane crashed in a snowstorm. Everyone on the plane was killed. If Ritchie had lived, he might have had a long career. He is remembered as a rocker who died long before his time.

Why do you think kids liked rock and roll better than their parents' music?

2 Hitsville and the Brits

"You say you want a revolution?"
— "REVOLUTION" BY THE BEATLES

In the early 60s, Motown Records in Detroit, Michigan, was turning out so many hits that it became known as Hitsville, U.S.A. Stars on this record label would top the charts again and again. Motown Records was home to the most successful girl group in history. This group was better than great. In fact, they were Supreme.

Meanwhile, in England, four young lads were getting ready to lead the British invasion.

The Supremes

The year was 1959. The place was the Brewster Housing Projects in Detroit. A group of girls got together. They called themselves the Primettes.

Berry Gordy Jr. thought the Primettes had a lot of talent. He was Motown's **founder.** But he told them to finish high school first. The group joined Motown after graduation. They changed their name to the Supremes.

At first, none of their records did very well. Then the Supremes were given a song called "Where Did Our Love Go?" The song was rejected by another girl group. They thought the song was silly. The Supremes didn't like the song either. But they sang it anyway. "Where Did Our Love Go?" went to number one. The Supremes had made it to the top of the charts!

The Supremes became one of the best-paid acts in the U.S. Onstage, the three young women wore beautiful matching clothes. Their dance moves were perfectly in synch.

Even their hairstyles were alike. Today, this style is still popular. Just look at groups like TLC and Destiny's Child.

After the group broke up, the lead singer, Diana Ross, went on to have a successful solo career that made her even more famous.

The Supremes went from rags to riches. So did four boys from England. Their names are John, Paul, George, and Ringo.

Left to right: Cindy Birdsong, Mary Wilson, and Diana Ross are the Supremes.

The Beatles

Pop stars have come and gone. Usually their fame lasts until they fall from the charts. A rare few never seem to fade away. Elvis is among the few. The Beatles are as well.

In the late 50s, four young men from Liverpool, England, formed a band. They were John Lennon, Paul McCartney, George Harrison, and Ringo Starr. They called themselves the Beatles. The Beatles were all big fans of early American rock and roll. Their first hits were simple love songs, like "I Wanna Hold Your Hand."

Girls screamed and fainted at the sight of the Beatles. Beatles' fan clubs were everywhere. Soon boys began to dress like the Beatles. They grew their hair long. The British press made up a word for the way Beatles fans' acted. They called it "Beatlemania." When the Beatles came to America, teens went wild.

John Lennon and Paul McCartney wrote most of the Beatles' songs. Their musical style changed as the years went by. Instead of simple

The Beatles wave to fans at London Airport in February, 1965. From left to right they are George, John, Ringo and Paul.

love songs, they sang about modern life and politics. But not all of their songs were serious. Some were funny, like "Yellow Submarine."

By the end of the 60s, the group was torn by disagreements. The band broke up in 1970. By that time they had sold more albums than any other music performers in history.

John, Paul, George, and Ringo all went on to have solo careers. Paul formed the band Wings with his wife Linda. Sadly, John was killed in 1980 by a crazed fan. But no one Beatle alone could come close to the fame that the group had achieved. Many people still consider them the most popular group in the history of rock and roll. Just ask your parents!

What group would you consider the most popular in history?

3 Small Screen Gems

"C'mon get happy."
— *THE PARTRIDGE FAMILY* THEME

During the 70s, disco and punk rock divided music fans. Young people no longer listened to one kind of music. But they all could agree on one thing—TV. That's where the most popular teen idols could be found. The Fonz from *Happy Days*, *The Brady Bunch* kids, and *Charlie's Angels* were just a few.

But one TV star also made it to the top of the charts. It was the pop star David Cassidy from the popular TV show *The Partridge Family*. He became the biggest teen idol of his time.

Photo: Henry Dilitz/Corbis

David Cassidy was too famous to live a normal life.

David Cassidy

Can you imagine your family as a pop band? That was the idea behind the hit TV show *The Partridge Family*. *The Partridge Family* was a sitcom about a mom and her five kids who formed a band. They toured the country in a brightly-painted school bus. They were just your normal, average family—in concert.

The Partridge Family starred David Cassidy. David played Keith, the oldest brother. Most of the Partridges **lip-synched** and pretended to play their instruments. But David was a musician. He sang lead vocals on all the show's songs. "I Think I Love You" became a number one song in 1970.

The Partridge Family aired for four seasons and released four albums. During that time, David Cassidy kept up a grueling schedule. He filmed the show by day and flew around the country giving concerts by night. His picture was on the cover of every teen magazine.

David's fans followed him wherever he went. Once he was rushed to the hospital. A guard had to be put outside of his room. Otherwise, David's fans would have mobbed his bedside!

David was trapped by his fame. He wanted to be able to live a normal life. But as long as he remained a teen idol, that was impossible. When *The Partridge Family* went off the air, David was almost relieved.

Meanwhile, another group made up of real brothers was rocketing up the charts.

The Jackson 5

They were one of the most loved family groups in pop music. Their first four songs hit number one on the music charts. They even had their own cartoon.

The Jackson 5 was made up of the brothers Jackie, Tito, Marlon, Jermaine, and Michael. The Jacksons were a musical family. All eleven members could sing and dance. The five eldest Jackson brothers began performing in their home town of Gary, Indiana. They competed in talent shows. They opened for other musical acts. People loved the Jackson brothers—especially the youngest, Michael.

Michael was the lead singer. He had a high, clear voice. And he was an amazing dancer.

The Jackson 5 released their first single in 1969. It was called "I Want You Back." It went straight to number one. The record quickly sold over two million copies. At the time, Jackie was 18, Tito was 16, Jermaine was 15, Marlon was 12, and Michael was 11.

The early 70s were busy years. The Jackson

Michael Jackson in 1975, singing and dancing with the Jackson 5.

5 cartoon was popular on Saturday morning TV. And the boys kept putting out hits. Fans screamed, cried, and followed them wherever they went. Fan magazines like *Right On!* ran their picture on cover after cover. In addition, Michael released his first solo album in 1971, *Got to Be There*.

By 1975, the Jackson brothers had been at the top of the charts for many years. They had fame, success, and the love of fans around the world. The boys felt ready to take control of their destiny. Up until now, Motown **producer** Berry Gordy Jr. had been in charge. One brother, Jermaine, decided to strike out on his own. The remaining brothers changed their name to The Jacksons.

The brothers got a new name, but they kept their old magic. Their albums *Destiny, Triumph,* and *Victory* were all big hits. In 1984, The Jacksons went on the Victory tour. That was the last project that featured Michael. By then he was a superstar all by himself. And his fame would make David Cassidy look like an unknown.

Why do you think some stars feel trapped by fame?

Music + Television

"I want my MTV!"
— COMMERCIAL FOR **MTV**

Something exciting happened to music in the 80s. MTV was born. MTV, short for music television, played videos of hit songs. The video might show a hot new band performing. Or, it might be like a collage or a mini-movie.

Michael Jackson was the decade's biggest star, and his videos are still considered among the best ever made. Another megastar was born during the 80s, and she's still going strong.

Michael Jackson

After Michael left the Jacksons, his solo career took off. In 1979, Michael made the album *Off the Wall*. It made him a superstar. People thought Michael could not get any hotter. They were wrong.

In 1982, Michael made *Thriller*. The album lived up to its name. It sold more than 51 million copies worldwide. It won eight Grammy awards. It became the most successful record of all time.

The videos from *Thriller* helped to make the album the huge hit that it was. And the videos for "Billie Jean," "Beat It," and "Thriller" helped make MTV even more popular. The videos showed Michael's amazing dance moves. But the video for the song "Thriller" was really special. It was like a scary mini-movie. It even had special effects.

By 1984, Michael had become "The King of Pop." Fans imitated his styles. Everyone started doing the "moonwalk," a dance that Michael made popular. People also copied his trademark—a glittery white glove. Michael said it showed the magic of his onstage life—the life he had led since he was a small child.

Offstage, it was hard for Michael to live like a regular person. Fans and photographers followed him everywhere. Michael couldn't visit a store or amusement park without causing a riot. And this was true all over the world.

Michael Jackson became one of the most famous people on the planet. But he paid for it by giving up a normal life.

Michael Jackson performs a charity concert in 1999, wearing his trademark glove.

Madonna

Some people would hate the kind of fame that becomes a prison. But this woman wanted as much fame as she could get. She started her music career in the 80s. She became one of the most famous—and powerful—women in the music industry…ever.

She was born Madonna Ciccone, but she's known worldwide as simply Madonna. Although she's a megastar now, no one took her seriously at first. People made fun of the unusual clothes she wore. They accused her of having no talent. But Madonna has never worried too much about what other people say.

Madonna was born in Michigan. She moved to New York City in 1978. Her dream was to be a dancer. But Madonna sang, too. Her first hit, "Everybody," became a hit in dance clubs. She recorded her first album *Madonna* in 1983. But it was her videos that really got people's attention. Madonna had a style that screamed, "Look at me!"

Soon young girls everywhere started

In 1998, Madonna had her hands painted with henna tattoos.

dressing like Madonna. The press made up a name for these fans. They called them "wanna-be's." Maybe that's why Madonna has changed her look so often. She needed to stay one step ahead of the pack she created! Her hair went from long to short. Then it went from platinum blond to black.

Recently, Madonna became a mother for the second time. But that may be the only thing she's ever repeated. People can't wait to see what she'll do next. And that may be part of the secret to her success.

How did MTV help pop stars reach the top of the charts?

Spice of Life

"Tell me what you want, what you really, really want."

— **"WANNABE" SUNG BY THE SPICE GIRLS**

In the 90s, music came in many flavors. Grunge was born in Seattle, Washington, and became popular throughout the country. Hip hop grew more popular than ever.

But the 90s were special for another reason. For the first time since the 60s, female performers were taking center stage. Five "spicy" girls from England were about to conquer the world (for a little while).

And they weren't the only spicy things around. The other big news in music was a hot new Latin beat.

The Spice Girls are (top row) Sporty, Baby, (bottom row) Ginger, Scary, and (right) Posh.

The Spice Girls

In 1996, a song called "Wannabe" hit the radio. It played constantly. The group that made this song became a music sensation. They were the Spice Girls.

A man named Chris Herbert came up with the idea. Chris wanted to create an all-girl group. He **auditioned** 400 girls from dance and drama schools all around England. He chose five. They were Geri Halliwell, Mel C (for Chisolm), Mel B (for Brown), Victoria Adams, and Emma Bunton.

Each girl picked a nickname. The red-headed Geri became Ginger Spice. Athletic Mel C became Sporty Spice. The dramatic Mel B became Scary Spice. Classy Victoria became Posh Spice. And girlish Emma became Baby Spice.

The Spice Girls wore flashy clothes. They danced on sky-high platform shoes. They sang songs that spread their message of "girl power." Fans loved it. They could not get enough of the Spice Girls.

Soon the Spice Girls were on posters,

buttons, key chains, stickers, candy wrappers, a video game, and more. Stores could not keep Spice Girls products on their shelves. The girls even made a movie called *Spice World*.

The fame of the Spice Girls died down as the 90s ended. First Geri left the band. Then Mel B and Victoria both married and became moms. The group lasted for only a few short years. But while they were on top, the Spice Girls were the hottest girl band ever.

Will Smith

The theme song starts: "In West Philadelphia born and raised…" The show is *The Fresh Prince of Bel-Air*. It went on TV in 1990. And it became an instant hit. Its star Will Smith was already famous as a rapper. He had a huge hit with the song "Parents Just Don't Understand." As a rapper he was known as the Fresh Prince.

Will was nicknamed "Prince" by a high school teacher. He got this name because of his royal attitude. Will added the "Fresh" later.

When Will was 16, he met a DJ named Jeff Townes. They called themselves "DJ Jazzy Jeff and the Fresh Prince." Will and Jeff performed at parties. They became so popular that they started to make records.

It was Will's music fame that got him a job on TV. But it was his talent as a comic actor that kept him there. Soon Will began to get parts in movies. During the 90s, he appeared in eight

The Fresh Prince, Will Smith, with his pal DJ Jazzy Jeff.

films, including *Men in Black, Independence Day,* and *Wild, Wild West.* Will became a megastar. But even with all that going on, Will continued to turn out hit songs. "Getting Jiggy Wit It," "Miami," and "Just the Two of Us" are just a few of them.

Amazing as all this success has been, it has not changed Will. He stayed the easy-going, funny guy fans first fell in love with. Happily married and a devoted dad, this Prince is a regular nice guy!

Ricky Martin

Latin music has always had its loyal fans. But by the end of the 90s, nearly everyone was shaking their hips to a Latin beat.

Ricky Martin began his career in the boy band Menudo. These Puerto Rican teens found fame around the world during the 80s. Like the Spice Girls, Menudo was created by a producer with an eye for talent.

Ricky moved to Mexico after he left Menudo. He kept singing. He also acted on a

Ricky Martin entertaining his fans at a concert in Madrid, Spain during his "Livin' la vida loca" tour.

Photo: © Reuters Media/Corbis

Mexican soap opera. Ricky made a few albums in Spanish. Then he moved to the U.S. He landed a part on the popular daytime soap opera *General Hospital.*

Soon Ricky's musical career began to heat up too. His song "La copa de la vida" became the 1998 World Cup theme song.

Next, Ricky made his first English-language album. The song "Livin' la vida loca" was on it. That song became the biggest-selling number one single in the history of Columbia Records.

In February, 1999 more than a billion viewers watched Ricky perform at the Grammys. Ricky's career is in high gear. In addition to winning the Grammy, he won two Billboard Awards, sold millions of records, and embarked on a tour that's taken him to four continents. Ricky says he wants to sing and perform forever. His fans hope his wish comes true!

What do you think makes some songs popular?

The New Kids

"Hit me, baby, one more time."
— **"BABY ONE MORE TIME" SUNG BY BRITNEY SPEARS**

Today's hit makers are not very different from those of the past. They are talented, good-looking, and young—very young. They include soloists like Britney Spears and Christina Aguilera and boy groups such as *NSYNC and the Backstreet Boys.

The good news is that these young stars may be around for a long time to come. That is, with any luck, they will. For now anyway, they have made it to the top of the charts.

Britney Spears in concert during 1999.

Britney Spears

Britney Spears began her career at age eight. By that time, she was already acting, singing, and dancing professionally. At 11, she got a part on *The New Mickey Mouse Club*. That show was to become a teen-idol machine. On that show, Britney shared the stage with other soon-to-be pop sensations Christina Aguilera and *NSYNC members Justin Timberlake and J.C. Chasez.

After leaving *The New Mickey Mouse Club* Britney recorded her mega-hit album *Baby, One More Time.* To **promote** the album, she sang, danced, and gave out copies of her CD in malls across America. Then the video hit MTV, and the rest is history.

Britney first toured as the opening act for *NSYNC. *NSYNC's Justin Timberlake was a former mouseketeer just like Britney. Now they have something else in common. In September of 2000, Britney confirmed that Justin is her boyfriend.

Britney's second album, *Ooops! I Did It Again,* was another smash hit. This time Britney has a new, grown-up look and sound. Britney said that she wants to keep growing and changing, just like her idol. Yes, even pop stars have idols. Britney's idol is none other than Madonna.

Christina Aguilera

Christina Aguilera was also a child star. She appeared on TV's *Star Search* at age eight. At 10, she sang the national anthem at pro football and hockey games. At age 12, she too joined *The New Mickey Mouse Club*. After leaving the show, she headed overseas to become a star.

First, Christina made a splash in Japan. Then she almost caused a riot in Romania. She went into a crowd during her concert. And fans went wild.

Back in the States, Christina got her big break. She sang the theme song for the animated movie, *Mulan*. The song became a hit. People said Christina reminded them of superstars like Mariah Carey and Whitney Houston.

Christina's first album was a huge success. The album had several hot songs like "Genie in a Bottle," and "I Turn to You." Christina's videos were red-hot, too.

Christina has been offered parts in movies.

But, for now, she wants to stay with her first love, music. Christina says that her life is a dream come true.

Christina Aguilera poses in a Chicago park in 1999.

Backstreet Boys

A.J. McLean, Howie Dorough, Nick Carter, Kevin Richardson, and Brian Littrell started out small. They played **gigs** at high school dances and at Sea World but all that has changed. Now they play to screaming mobs worldwide.

Photo: © Ethan Miller/Corbis

The Backstreet Boys are, from left to right; Nick, Howie, Brian, A.J., and Kevin.

Like Christina Aguilera, the Backstreet Boys first hit it big outside the country. They were stars in Europe in the mid 90s. Boy bands were popular there. In 1997, the Backstreet Boys won MTV Europe's Viewer's Choice Award.

But soon, the Backstreet Boys found success back in the U.S., too. Before long, they could not go anywhere without security guards. Once two fans hid in the storage bin of their tour bus. Another time, someone climbed a barbed-wire fence to get into their dressing room.

The Backstreet Boys were on the fast track to fame. In less than three years, they sold over 55 million records. Their megahit "I Want It That Way" was number one in more than 16 countries around the world.

The Backstreet Boys have grown used to life as famous pop stars. But they do not take their fans' love for granted. They know that hot young bands can come and go. And they'd like to stick around for a long time.

*NSYNC

The group *NSYNC formed during the late 90s. It all began when J.C. Chasez and Justin Timberlake wanted to start a group. Then Chris Kirkpatrick, Joey Fatone, and Lance Bass joined. And *NSYNC was born.

Like the Backstreet Boys, *NSYNC also found their first taste of success in Europe. But it didn't take long for them to be discovered back at home. Their pop sound and slick dance moves won them even more fans.

Soon teen magazines like *Tiger Beat* and *Girls' Life* were putting pictures of *NSYNC on their covers. Fans couldn't get enough facts about their favorite band. They found out that J.C. loved Chinese food. Justin's nickname was Curly. Chris's dream girl was Gwen Stefani of the band No Doubt. Joey loved tacos and pizza. Lance's last name really was Bass.

*NSYNC has a lot in common with the Backstreet Boys. But the bands do not feel jealous of each other. Many fans love both bands. After all, you can't get enough good music.

Photo: © Dorothy Low/Corbis-Outline

*NSYNC are, from left to right: Chris, Joey, J.C., Lance, and Justin.

Who do you think will be the next big thing at the top of the charts?

Glossary

auditioned did a short performance to win a part in a play, concert, etc.

contract a legal agreement between people or companies

founder a person who sets up or starts something

gigs jobs for a musician or a band to play music in public

lip-synched moved the lips in synch with recorded sound to seem as if performing it

producer the person in charge of raising money, hiring people, and generally supervising the making of an album, play, movie, or TV program

promote to make the public aware of something or someone